May First

The day an ordinary Times Square street vendor helped thwart a terrorist attack.

A True Story

By

MR. DUANE MELVIN JACKSON SR.

With Ms. Sheila Banks

ISBN: 1463676816
ISBN 13: 9781463676810

This book is dedicated to the women in my life: my Mother, my Mother-in-Law, and my Wife.

Duane Jackson's journey on May 1, 2010 from his vendor table at 45th and Broadway to a parked, explosives-packed car was but a few steps away. The fact is these same few steps were deeply rooted in times since long since passed yet destined to play a role in the decisions Duane made that fateful day. Had Duane not been nurtured by the care and upbringing of his family and instilled with a sense of duty to his country and community while in the military and through the turbulent times of the early 70s I submit Duane may not have been as prepared as in deed as he was.

It is said that the roles of husband, father and friend often serve to sharpen one's sense of responsibility and purpose. Clearly, Duane was no exception. By his quick and unselfish actions, Duane served to defy the intent of a terrorist who was hell-bent on doing great harm to many people who offered no ill-will.

By his actions, Duane reminded each of us of just how important it is to "say something" when you "see something". With each unwavering step toward that pending explosion Duane demonstrated a willingness to "do something" as well. Times Square is still Times Square thanks to Duane's readiness to "see", "say" and "do" what needed to be done.

With gratitude and thanks;

Richard Morris, President, Decision-gates

☆ ☆ ☆

May First is a riveting account of the events in Times Square that stunned America. Duane Jackson's vigilance has transformed the New York born expression *"If you see something, say something"* into a national campaign against terrorism.

Bruce L. DeBon, Managing Director, Diversified Security Solutions, Inc.

☆ ☆ ☆

I've known Duane "Smokey" Jackson on the other side of 35 years. He has always been a modern day "swashbuckler," an unstoppable visionary, and a man for all seasons. Be it organizing, networking or saving Times Square from imminent ruin...his story is one to be heard.

Bus Howard (college roommate)

☆ ☆ ☆

"When I look at Duane Smokey Jackson, I see a loving husband and father. I see an astute businessperson and a patriotic veteran. When I worked with Duane at the FBI/New York Office Citizens' Academy Alumni Association his integrity, tenacity and creativity made it easy for us to work together for our community. I happened to be in NYC Times Square when Duane "saw something and said something" about that car bomb meant to kill us all. Thus, when I look at Duane I see one word – courage! Thus, I recommend that all read Duane's inspired message so you too will know what you see and what to say."

The Honorable JoLinda Ruth Cogen

Past President
New York Office/FBI Citizens' Academy Alumni Association NYO/FBICAAT)

Visit
www.DuaneSmokeyJackson.com
to access links to publications, videos, interviews,
testimonials, and current updates.

Foreword

I first met Duane Jackson when I spoke at the prestigious FBI, New York Office, Citizens' Academy. It was a routine presentation for me, but my meeting with Duane was anything but routine. His sincerity and humility over his heroic actions were qualities that immediately made you take notice of him and qualities that forged a genuine friendship based on mutual respect.

As that friendship developed, I learned more about the man that is credited for saving Times Square. His service in the US Navy during the Vietnam era, the importance of family, and his sense of community and giving back, make Duane someone you want to know. These are just a few of the remarkable facets of his character, but they all contributed to his actions in New York City on May 1, 2010. Actions that helped avert a catastrophe that would have a serious impact on Times Square, New York, and The United States of America.

"Why get involved?" was a familiar expression on the lips of many prior to that frightening day. Thankfully Duane's emergency training in the Navy and his presence on Wall Street for both attacks on the World Trade Center gave him a heightened sense of awareness that inspired his quotation, "See something, say something" and because of that mantra he instinctively and without hesitation dove into action. Have you ever been to 45th Street and Broadway on any given Saturday? Do you know how many people walk on one of the busiest streets in New York? Can you imagine the amount of business a vendor transacts with the throngs of tourists, theatergoers, and city dwellers passing his stand? Who has time to notice a car that is running, parked on the corner with emergency lights on, keys in the ignition, and no driver? Someone who has been trained to protect our citizens, someone who puts safety first, someone who had the good sense to say something when what he was seeing just didn't add up. Someone like Duane Jackson. Knowing something was wrong and reporting his suspicion to a nearby police officer, Duane "said something." The NYPD did an outstanding job in securing the area, getting the bomb squad on scene, contacting the FBI, and finally rendering the area safe. The FBI together with the NYPD captured the terrorist, Faisal Shahzad, within a few days averting what could have been a disaster of cataclysmic proportions.

On September 25, 2011, New York City Police Department Commissioner, Raymond Kelly, was interviewed on *60 Minutes* regarding his Counter-Terrorism Bureau's response to the Times Square attempted bombing. During that interview Commissioner Kelly stated, "it was because we were lucky" that disaster was averted, "and we'll take luck anytime," but with all due respect Commissioner Kelly, luck had nothing to do with it, we had Duane Jackson, and we'll take him anytime!

Joaquin "Jack" Garcia

Retired Special Agent of the FBI and Author of *Making Jack Falcone: An Undercover FBI Agent Takes Down a Mafia Family*

Table of Contents

Co-Author's Note

MAY FIRST is the story of an ordinary man who found himself faced with extraordinary circumstances. It is the first person account of Duane Jackson, the Times Square street vendor who spotted the explosive-laden SUV, alerting police, thus helping to foil the terrorist plot to blow up Times Square.

MAY FIRST is the story of a man who does not consider himself a hero; although his heroic act helped prevent a catastrophe that could have taken thousands of lives, including his own. Heroes are not born. They evolve and they fight and conquer personal demons to become the people they are meant to be.

MAY FIRST is a story for all peace-loving Americans and people all over the world; any American whose life has been touched by a veteran or any member of the active armed services – and for anyone who loves a hero. Even a reluctant one. God Bless us, everyone.

Sheila Banks

Preface

When I was a kid, May 1st meant spring and that summer fun was not far away. It meant May Day celebrations and flowers and the Maypole. How life has changed. On May 1, 2011, our Commander-In-Chief informed Americans and citizens of the world that the most wanted, notorious terrorist on the planet was dead. Under the direction of President Barack Obama, Navy Seals Special Forces took out Osama bin Laden at his compound in Abbottabod, Pakistan.

One year previously to the date, the threat of terrorism against our country was right in my face. Literally. I fall to my knees in gratitude each and everyday that on May 1, 2010, I had the presence of mind to question the illegally parked, vacant dark green SUV sitting not more than ten feet from my vendor stand in Times Square; packed with enough explosives to annihilate the entire area. Plotted by a naturalized American citizen, Faisal Shahzad.

I have operated my vending business at 45th and Broadway for 14 years. I fall to my knees in gratitude each and every day that on May 1st of 2010, I was able to do my small part to help New Yorkers and Americans dodge a terrible bullet. The rest, as they say, is history. A good piece of history, Thank God. This is my story of what happened that day to me, an ordinary guy. A veteran. A father and husband. A businessman. An American.

Chapter One

Dodged a Bullet

I t didn't hit me until five weeks later, the first night of the FBI Citizens' Academy Class. Special Agent Greg Fowler, the FBI agent in charge of counterterrorism, was addressing the 44 men and women who had been hand-picked for this prestigious 10 week-long program.

"The FBI replicated the events of May 1," he began; setting us up for the DVD we were going to preview. The FBI simulation DVD was to be released to the media the next day because the bomber, Faisal Shahzad, was to be sentenced then. "We rigged an SUV, another Nissan Pathfinder; identical to the one Shahzad parked on 45th and Broadway. We loaded it up with the same crude explosive materials, but we used a different fuse."

Agent Fowler paused and looked at me. "Duane, we placed cardboard cutouts all around the area. We marked where you would have been standing. Had those explosives detonated the way Shahzad planned, the blast would have been devastating. The force would have demolished everyone and everything within 75 yards in four directions and up three stories."

The proverbial chill ran down my spine. For a moment, I couldn't breathe. I thought I might even be sick, and I'm not a faint-of-heart kind of guy. *Oh my God, my mind screamed. I could have died, along with thousands of other innocent people. The bastard wanted to kill us!* The reality finally slapped me upside the head. The S.O.B. could have killed *me*!

Although my actual mortality didn't sink in until Agent Fowler brought it home at the FBI Citizens Academy, the one emotion I *had* experienced after "the incident" was anger. It rushed back this night. Came bubbling right back up to the surface. I was really pissed off all over again, and had to fight off one single thought: to give that cowardly mothhaf**ka a New York beat-down!

May 1, 2010

It was a glorious, gorgeous spring day. One of those days that are so pretty you just can't wait to jump out of bed and hit the ground running to soak it all up! Happy to be alive! Clear blue skies. Pleasantly warm, no humidity. Perfect.

Even at 8:00 in the morning, that particular Saturday was different; busier than most. Not only were myself and the other food, drink and accessory vendors throughout the area gearing up for the vibrant onslaught of activity and the lifeblood of New York City known as tourists – but it was the morning of the 17th annual Revlon Run/Walk for Breast Cancer.

More than 40,000 men, women, children and entire families were registered to participate in the event, which kicked off from Times Square at 9:00 a.m. With that kind of mega-event going on, you can't set up as close to the corner as you would like. So, I positioned my stand at 45th Street just a little further up the block. Didn't matter. Spring was in the air and all was well with the world. Besides, I had a bird's eye view of the celebrity opening ceremony, starring Halle Berry, Jessica Alba, and Jessica Biel. I remember thinking, *Could this day get any better?* Well, ok, to be fair, there were male celebrities too - Dr. Mehmet Oz, Jesse L. Martin and Trey Songz.

Business was plentiful that first day of May and most folks seemed to be in high spirits. That afternoon and early evening, there was a DJ set up in front of Sunglass Hut, which is directly in front of me on the corner of 45th and Broadway. He was firing up the crowds with some spicy salsa. At least two hundred revelers were having a great time dancing and enjoying the music. They didn't mind the congestion on the sidewalk. It was a street party! Very festive, fun and very New York.

I just happened to turn around and look south. I noticed a vehicle parked on the other side of the street that wasn't there just a few minutes before. I regularly keep a pretty vigilant eye – it *is* Times Square, after all, and where there are people, there are *other* people trying to rip off you or somebody else. But, this guy had left his Pathfinder parked in a bus turning lane where no one is allowed to park on 45th Street. This is a really narrow street anyway. I know, because I've had my truck hit twice by buses making that turn too short onto 45th Street.

The car was running and the flashers were on. I walked over and peeked inside the passenger side. The keys were inside. *Weird.* I quickly scanned the crowd, thinking maybe the guy had run into the bank to use an ATM or something. My first inclination was to open the door, reach inside, turn the car off and grab the keys. *But, something stopped me.* First, I saw that there weren't just a couple of keys on the ring in the ignition. There were maybe 15 – like a janitor's key ring. *Who the hell else carries that many damn keys around*? Plus, the back window and the back side windows were painted black. Not *tinted* black like you see on a lot of vehicles. Black *paint*.

I spotted and flagged down Officer Jason Miranda, one of the regular area beat cops, who was walking up the street. Jason pulled out his flashlight. As I shared with him that I didn't know where the guy who left this vehicle was, he was looking in from the driver's side. I was trying to peer in from the passenger side. At that point, the officer on horseback rode around and asked if the Pathfinder was my car. When we established that it wasn't, the first fuse went off. It sounded like the pop, pop, popping of firecrackers going off and gray smoke started oozing from the car.

The popping and the smoke startled all of us. I jumped back, thinking, *Uh-oh. This thing is really bad. This car is gonna blow.* Of course, at the time, I thought it was just a regular car that had badly overheated or something. The mounted officer started moving people back.

It was close to 6:45 p.m. Officers from the next block were the first responders. Throngs of tourists and New Yorkers were still shopping, milling about and enjoying the energy of the area on such a beautiful spring evening. Others were having dinner before heading to the theaters. The officers began evacuating the streets, stores and other businesses; moving everyone back and away for their own safety.

I moved my car from its usual spot near my stand close to the corner to further up the street, past my neighbor, the Marriot Marquis. Within minutes, dozens of fire trucks and police cars flooded the area. To me, it felt surreal, like watching a movie or an episode of *Law and Order* in slow motion. Or, under water. The reality was that everything was actually happening very quickly – so quickly it was mind-boggling. I was able to stay because I was a "witness" and was told authorities were going to want to speak with me again. Plus, all of my merchandise was still out on my fully re-stocked table.

As I think back on it, I recognize that God, a Higher Power or Whomever you believe in, was certainly with us that day. The firefighters leaped to action, jumping off their trucks, hauling their hoses behind them. After realizing they could not see into the back of the SUV, it was decided not to break the windows and shove the hose inside. Instead, members of the NYC Police Department's bomb squad were called in. Garbed head-to-toe in their special protective gear, the bomb squad shattered the Pathfinder's back windows and sent in what looked like some kind of robotic device to examine whatever was inside. We now know, of course, that propane canisters, gasoline cans, fertilizer, consumer grade fireworks and two clocks with batteries were hidden behind the black painted windows.

The yellow tape was thrown up, seemingly out of nowhere. My corner was officially a crime scene. I was questioned by authorities over and again. *Did I see who was driving the car? No. How did I notice the car? Did I have any idea how long the vehicle had been vacant?*

In the meantime, Times Square, one of the busiest and most heavily populated sections of New York City on *any* Saturday, was put on lockdown. From 43rd to 48th Street and from Sixth to 8th Avenue, several – but not all – theaters and stores were evacuated; as was the South Tower of the Marriot Marquis. The curtains on some Broadway shows went up 15 to 30 minutes late. Some, not at all. Theatergoers who were able to see their shows were directed to alternative exits.

I was finally allowed to leave around 4 a.m. Sunday morning. I live in Westchester County, 42 miles outside the city. My wife, Linda was up waiting for me. I don't think she felt the full impact of the situation either. At least, not immediately. She, of course, had seen the news coverage and was calling people, alerting them because "that's Duane's block." We had spoken on the phone, so she knew I was ok. When I got home, I guess I pretty much downplayed it myself, saying something like, "yeah, well, you know, some crazy guy had some explosive shit in his car. But, the cops got it."

I thought sleep would come easily because I was exhausted. But, my mind wouldn't stop bombarding me with questions and images. *Why didn't I see this guy get out of the car? He couldn't have been out of that car more than 2 or 3 minutes before I noticed it. Why didn't he park in the middle of the block? What if I hadn't noticed the car at all?*

chapter two

The Morning After

I was supposed to play golf that Sunday morning – my passion. But, even after sleeping for only about an hour, I decided that it was important to go back to my stand. *My* stand. My little corner of the world. I think it was my way of grasping for some sense of normalcy. Like too many Americans, certainly too many New Yorkers – I have witnessed terrorism in my city. Against my city. First, while working on Wall Street – just blocks away from the first attack on the World Trade Center back in February 1993, with the car bomb in the garage; and again on that terrible September day in 2001.

So, this Sunday, this second day of May, I headed in. I think I needed to help show that Times Square was open for business by me being open for business. I needed to show other New Yorkers and the world that New York City was open for business. That we were *alright*.

And, then they came.

First one, then two, then dozens. National media. Local media. International media from South America, China, Africa, Australia and throughout Europe. TV, radio, newspapers and magazines. ABC, NBC, CBS, FOX, MSNBC, CNN, the BBC, The *Tom Joyner Morning Show, Extra, Inside Edition*. Gayle King's producer came by the stand a few days later. While I never sat down with Lady O, I did enjoy a riveting hour-long discussion on terrorism with Gayle on her XM satellite radio show. I scored extra points for that one because my wife *loves* Gayle! But wow, man. Yeah, I admit it. This was all pretty heady stuff for an ordinary guy like me.

Sometime on Sunday, a producer from *Good Morning America* called wanting to book me and my entire family for the show Monday morning. Cool. Thing is, after speaking with me, the producer showed up at my home later that afternoon. I was in Times Square – not in Westchester - and thought everything was set. So, to my wife and me, the visit was a bit unexpected. Linda called me afterwards to let me know how visibly surprised the guy was to see where we lived. Guess he's still trying to figure out how a street vendor could afford to live in an attractive, four-bedroom home in Westchester.

For years, whenever anyone has had the nerve to ask me directly, I have always answered, "I married money," my pat response - which I always think is pretty funny. Don't know if Linda does.

Since I'm the one telling this story and hopefully have a captive audience, I'm going to grab this as an opportunity to encourage people to drop that old habit of judging and holding fast to stereotypes. So, let's dispel some myths right here. One of them being that a street vendor, especially a "disabled veteran" street vendor, can't possibly live well. (I sustained a back injury during my stint in the Navy.) As I hope I have remembered to share in most of the media interviews, I am a college graduate (Boston University) with post-graduate work in Urban Planning. I've worked in offices for both government and private industry. But as a street vendor, I am an independent businessman with virtually no overhead. (Smart, right?) My wife is a banker, and we've been pretty savvy investors. So, there you have it . . . careful about judging that book by its cover.

I also gained a little insight into how media works. After I agreed to the interview with ABC's *Good Morning America*, someone from Larry King's show called to ask if I could be on the program that Sunday night. The ABC guy who had been to my house came back down to 45th street and insisted that I *not* do Larry King. They wanted exclusivity. Apparently that's how the media game is played, and I had already given my word. You live and learn. By the way, there was no money involved in any of these interviews, as I never tried to sell my story to anyone. It never would have even occurred to me. When any outlet has offered money, I suggested they make a donation to Vietnam Veterans of America.

The questions from the media were pretty much the same, over and again.

When and how did you notice the car?

What about it made you suspicious?

Do you feel like a hero? The answer to that one is simple. No. I was simply in the right place at the right time for the right results. Heroes are those fearless Navy Seals who rid the world of Osama bin Laden, and Captain Chelsey "Sully" Sullenberger who safely landed US Airways Flight 1549 on the Hudson River on January 15, 2009, just 5 blocks from my stand. All 150 passengers made it off safely because of him. Heroes are Wesley Autrey, the New York construction worker and Navy veteran who threw his body on top of the young man who fell onto the subway at the 137th Street station in New York back in 2007. A lady on the platform held onto Autrey's two little girls while he covered Cameron Hollopeter's body with his own in a drainage ditch between the tracks. The train rolled right over them, but was so close it left grease stains on Autrey's cap.

Those are heroes. I think my reaction to the suspicious SUV boils down to my basic personality and my military training. First, I am not the type of person who panics. I am also a Navy veteran, having served during the Vietnam era. I think my intense Navy training on what to do in an emergency simply kicked in.

How does it feel knowing that you and hundreds, maybe thousands of others could have been killed? Again, I understood the enormity of the situation intellectually. But, in my gut, I just didn't connect to it. Maybe because it was too scary emotionally to digest. Maybe there was a dis-connect because the thing didn't detonate. For some reason, for me the reaction of fear and shock over what could have been was delayed; even as I told the story over and over again.

The local Westchester media interviewed my neighbors with questions like *what kind of neighbor is Duane?* And, *what do you think of your neighbor, the hero?*

Thankfully, all of the responses were positive. My favorite, though, is from the wife of one of our favorite couples, both in their 80s, with whom we have shared Christmas Eve. Her response, "Well, my husband is a World War II veteran. Duane is a veteran. And, I always feel safe around veterans." 'Nuff said.

People frequently ask me what my children think of their old man, what happened, and the subsequent attention. My daughter Tiffany is 27, and my son Duane is 16. I think they are both proud, even though they don't always come right out and say it. Linda and I have both worked to instill in our children a sense of responsibility for themselves and others; and the importance of integrity. I have tried to teach my children to never be afraid to get involved and to always remember that human beings are a community of one. So, I think this was a really good "real life" teaching-by-example lesson. Of course, because Duane is a teenaged boy, he gets totally embarrassed when anyone mentions that they saw his dad on TV.

There was one interview, however, that I think even impressed *him*! It was Nick Cannon (yes, Mariah Carey's husband). He hosts the *Nick Cannon Show* here in New York City on 92.5. His producer called to invite both me and Duane, Jr. on the show. The station and the program are geared to a young demographic, so I'm sure my having a teenager was the motivation. (And, that's fine with me. If I can positively impact young people, what a blessing. How could I ask for more than that?) The producer wanted us to come in person, but it was a school day; and I told him I really didn't want to take Duane out of school. He just said, "OK. Let's do it over the phone." We did.

At the close of the interview, Nick said, "You know, I give out the Nick Cannon Hero's Award. I'm gonna come down to Times Square next week to present one to you." And, he did. Entourage, cameras and all!

I particularly enjoyed the interview with the original sky jock, Tom Joyner on his nationally syndicated morning show (so named because he used to jet between Chicago and Dallas to host his morning and evening radio shows. That, of course, was long before technology became so sophisticated, making actual travel to appear on a show or attend a meeting damn near obsolete.)

As I look back, it's kind of funny how that came about. I hadn't heard the broadcast the Monday morning after the incident because even though the popular *Tom Joyner Morning Show* is syndicated in well over one hundred radio markets throughout the country; the show was not broadcast in the New York tri-state area until recently.

Apparently Joyner's comedian sidekick, Jay Anthony Brown was joking in a "bit" that "Dwayne Johnson had saved Times Square" on May 1st. It was funny because most of you might know that the famous Dwayne Johnson is perhaps better known as the wrestler-turned-actor, "The Rock."

To which Joyner reportedly retorted, "No, Fool! It was *Duane* Jackson, a street vendor. *Not* D-Wayne the wrestler." One of the producers decided to check it out and called me. Coincidentally, the producer had received her Masters Degree from Boston University. *Small world.* I am also the founder and president of the Golden Decade Foundation, a black Boston-area college and university alumni group that provides scholarship and networking support to our children. So, she and I got to know each other as fellow alums, not just as producer and booked guest.

I was a guest on the show the next morning. As a result of my conversation with his producer, my interview with Tom covered more ground than the May 1st incident. We discussed Vietnam in relation to the current conflict in Afghanistan. And, because Joyner is a longtime dedicated advocate of higher education for black youngsters, we spent considerable time discussing the work of the Golden Decade Foundation. I was so moved when he thanked me for "throwing back the rope" to help our kids.

As I said, at that time the *TJMS* wasn't broadcast in New York. That's why it was really heartening – and surprising - that so many black people approached me on my corner after the broadcast to say, "I heard you on Tom Joyner. Thank you for your service."

"Thank you for 'throwing back the rope.'"

Or, "I went to college in Boston. How do I get involved with the Golden Decade Foundation?"

"Thank you for being a hero." There's that word again.

chapter three

Hello, Mr. President

A couple of days after "the incident," two suited gentlemen showed up at the stand, flashed their IDs and asked me to come with them. I could have sworn they told me they were NYPD detectives who were taking me down to the precinct to look at pictures. Which I thought was odd, because I repeated over and again that I never saw the guy. But, I got into the car nonetheless.

When we arrived at our destination, I knew something was up. This was no police precinct. It was a rundown, non-descript building in the old meat packing district.

Once inside, we were met by two other gentlemen, one being Special Agent Greg Fowler, the FBI agent in charge of counterterrorism. "You know, Mr. Jackson. We got you down here under false pretenses."

My spider senses started tingling, but I didn't panic, simply asking, "Why? What happened? What's going on?"

Special Agent Fowler graciously gestured for me to follow him. "Come on into the conference room. President Obama would like to speak with you."

Are you kidding me?

Again, it felt like being in the middle of a movie. Except these guys hadn't thrown the requisite sack over my head or blindfold me before forcing me into the car against my will. In retrospect, I guess the agents who picked me up couldn't exactly reveal their intent in the middle of Times Square.

I sat in a sparse but comfortable, modern-looking room at a conference table with nothing on it except a plain, disc-looking thing which turned out to be the phone speaker. The room was only decorated with an American flag and a New York State flag.

During the 15 minutes or so we waited for the President to come on the line, I struck up a conversation with Special Agent Fowler and Richard Krekol, Public Relations officer for the FBI. Somehow the conversation turned to gangs and how the first commandment among gang members and way too many kids is "don't snitch." Everybody hates a snitch. They told me how one enterprising group of young men even sold "Stop Snitching" tee shirts. Now, while I firmly believe that the whole "don't snitch" thought pattern is ignorant as hell; I must say "I ain't mad at 'em" on the entrepreneurial side.

"Yeah, the whole notion of not snitching is b.s.," one of the agents commented, adding, "Countless lives might have been lost on May 1st if you weren't what these knuckleheads call a 'snitch.'"

We were then informed that the President was on the line. Even though it was a very basic exchange, I couldn't believe that the President of the United States had asked to speak with *me*! President Obama thanked me "for my vigilance on behalf of the American people." He asked me what I sold. I told him ... women's pocketbooks, scarves, golf clubs. (I totally blew the opportunity to ask him if he would be interested in a round of golf with me sometime. Well, maybe after he reads this. So, somebody get him a copy, ok?) Before we ended the conversation, President Obama suggested I get Mayor Bloomberg to "buy the whole table when he comes by 'cause he's got it like that." Even though he is the leader of the free world and our badass Commander-In-Chief, our president still manages to relate to us regular folk as a normal guy.

After the call, the agents and I took some pictures. Outside, I declined their offer to give me a ride back; opting instead to get myself back to 45th and Broadway in a cab. As soon as I settled into the seat, the phone rang. It was a slightly annoyed producer at MSNBC asking, "Are you coming?"

"Excuse me?" Wow, I had forgotten that I was scheduled for an interview with MSNBC and apologized, explaining that I had been picked up by the FBI to take a call from the President.

She was like, "What? Wait. Hold on. It's coming over the AP right now." A brief pause. "Ok. So, here's what we're going to do. We're going to patch you right in to the studio. They're going to ask you what the president said and what you said. Ok? You ready?" I guess I was.

Meanwhile, the mega-sized ticker crawl in Times Square also carried the news that "President Obama called Times Square Vendor." *Me, Duane*

Jackson! I didn't see it; but, I certainly heard about it! What an age we live in. And, how humbled I am by the honor; an experience that will stay with me as long as I continue to draw breath.

Duane speaking with President Obama via phone just days after the incident on May 1ss when he saw something, and said something.

chapter_four

Who Saw It First?

My fellow vendor and disabled Vietnam vet Lance L. Orton has also been credited with spotting the SUV that Saturday. In subsequent interviews he has said, "There can't be two heroes. I don't want anyone riding on my story."

I can only tell what happened to me. What I saw; what I did.

It's almost funny that a week and a half after the incident, I learned that there was a third guy claiming he saw the car first. Alioune B. Niasse from Senegal. Niasse told the media that he started to call 911 when he spotted the Pathfinder, but that Lance urged him to instead alert the mounted officer. Frankly, I never saw Niasse; so I don't know where he came from. Whether this guy saw the car first or not – I have no idea. All three of us have received props. President Obama called Lance, too. He appeared on the Today Show and gave other interviews as well. And, bottom line – *we're still here*! The good guys won that day!

A few days after the event, a rep from the NY Mets called to say the organization would like to honor both Lance and me at a game. Lance and I were both recognized with a standing ovation during a Mets game against the San Francisco Giants at Citi Stadium. *A standing ovation*. Man! I had to pinch myself to make sure this was really happening. I can only assume that Lance felt the same sense of grateful exhilaration. As a longtime Mets fan, I cannot adequately express how amazing that experience was.

Or, how humbling.

Chapter Five

The 15 Minutes of Fame Turns Into an Hour

This was crazy. Almost overwhelming. More phone calls were received; tributes, accolades and proclamations were bestowed by Mayor Michael Bloomberg, then-Governor David Patterson, the New York City Council, and the New York State Assembly. *Really*? For having common sense? My neighbor, the Marriott Marquis graciously held a luncheon in my honor. Somehow, being recognized by one's peers – in my case, other Times Square business owners – is especially sweet. I was bowled over again when another neighbor, gorgeous model-turned-lifestyle guru-turned-restaurateur, Barbara "B" Smith, picked up the tab for my entire party and presented me with a "Thank You" gift certificate at her elegant B. Smith's at 8th Avenue and 46th Street one evening following "the incident."

I remain humbled by tributes from the Westchester County Board of Legislators, the Town of Cortlandt and the Village of Buchanan. Schools have invited me to deliver their graduation addresses.

Because of the events of May 1, 2010, I was also honored with the American Legion's prestigious Patriots

Award, the Vietnam Veterans Memorial Fund American Patriot Award (received at the Vietnam Memorial in Washington on Memorial Day, sitting next to the Chairman of the Joint Chiefs of Staff, Admiral Mike Mullins), the

Hendrick Hudson School District Citizenship Award and the NOBLE (National Organization of Black Law Enforcement Executives) *Man of the Year Award.*

Next to receiving a phone call from the President of the United States, possibly the most surprising and humbling experience was being included in *Time Magazine's 2010 Person of the Year* issue. My fellow vendors, Lance and Alioune were also included; the three of us appear in the same picture.

In addition to being grateful for these accolades and invitations, I can only pray to God that I am deserving; and that I can use these incredible opportunities for further good - as a platform for service to others.

The simple act of "seeing something and saying something" has afforded me the opportunity to address groups across the country, allowing me to share my voice on that which has been close to my heart for years – Veterans' rights; especially the rights of disabled veterans. I have long been an advocate of veteran's rights as founder and president of the New York Chapter of Vietnam Veterans of America for 18 years, a 21-year member of Disabled American Veterans and a 17 year member of the American Legion.

We know that the Lord moves in mysterious ways. For the appearance on *Good Morning America* following "the incident," I made a conscious decision to wear my American Legion hat (which I'd had for several years but only wore on Veterans Day) rather than my usual baseball cap. *Something just told me to.*

My wife, son, daughter and I had spent the night in a great suite at the Millennium Hotel in NYC so we could all be available the next morning to do the show right across the street in front of ABC. The air was charged with excitement; yet, that night, I remained eerily serene. Not scared or nervous; just calm.

Out of nowhere, the famous Norman Rockwell painting depicting a patriotic old guy watching a parade from the sidelines, wearing his American Legion hat, flashed in my mind.

Something told me that wearing this particular hat on national TV would have a deep meaning for anyone watching who had a father, grandfather, sibling or spouse who served in the armed forces, or who was also a member of the American Legion.

Coincidentally – or not – one of the Legionnaires from New York was on a business trip that day. This is how he told the story to me. "I stepped out of the shower, turned on the TV and saw you with that American Legion hat on. I almost fell off the bed in the hotel room. You're a hero, man, and here you were one of our guys! So, I got on the phone immediately and called the state president."

They tracked me down – not difficult to do. Next thing I knew, I was invited to address thousands of other veterans of many wars at the 92nd National Convention of the American Legion in Milwaukee in August of 2010; following General Erik Shinseki, Secretary of the U.S. Department of Veterans Affairs and Defense Secretary Robert Gates! Me – a regular guy! A street vendor! Only in America, right?

On May 3rd I was back to working at the corner of 45th and 7th Ave. That afternoon a gentleman approached my table and asked if I was Duane Jackson. He introduced himself as Bruce DeBon, the Managing Director of a local company called Diversified Security Solutions, Inc. He explained to me that the company was engaged in emergency preparedness and conducted trainings and drills in New York High Rise buildings. In the aftermath of 9-11 New York created a Local Law that required Commercial Office Buildings to create a non-fire related Emergency Action Plan. After filing the Plan with the New York City Fire Department certain Building Staff and Tenants were required to be trained. These trainings helped building occupants to know what to do, and what not to do, in the event of a host of possible emergencies in their building. Mr. DeBon explained that the underlying theme of all their trainings was to be vigilant, and to be aware. He looked at me and said "you are the poster child of vigilance and awareness", would you like to come and work with us? The following day I met him in his office and was introduced to two of the company's leading Directors. Mr. Richard McGill, a retired Lieutenant from the New York City Fire Department and Mr. Tom Calkins, a retired FDNY Captain. I knew immediately that I wanted to be a part of this team. In the months to follow I would attend Training sessions that are organized to help the volunteer Wardens in buildings understand the importance of being aware. After the mandated training either Mr. McGill or Mr. Calkins would introduce me to the room and I was typically met with a standing ovation. Little did I know then what an impact my vigilance had on so many people because I saw something, and I said something.

Chapter Six

Our Brothers' Keepers

May 1, 2010 changed my life forever. All I did was "say something because I saw something." That simple act and the subsequent experiences have made me realize now more than ever that *we are indeed our brothers' keepers.*

I thank God that the speaking opportunities continue; that people still think I have something to say. I thank God for the opportunity to speak to the hearts and minds of freedom-loving people in New York, America and throughout the world with this key message: We are all connected and responsible for each other.

We must all be vigilant, work together and realize that the things that divide us are not nearly as powerful as the things that unite us. We must exercise a heightened sense of awareness as we fight this new, common enemy of ours called terrorism.

Perhaps the scariest part is the realization that we continue to "grow" those who loathe this country – and loathe us - right here in our own back yard.

We must be on alert because sadly, chances are that the next terrorist attack on American soil will be executed by a westernized, assimilated Jihadist. People who are walking among us now. Drinking scotch. Womanizing. Maybe even have a DUI. They are American citizens. Raised as anyone else – a Southern Baptist, a Methodist, Lutheran or Catholic. Home grown. Going to school. Camouflaged to look and sound just like you and me.

Yet, somehow *we must remember that Muslim and terrorist are not synonymous.* Just as being Arab American and terrorist are not synonymous. What is it going to take to pound that into our dangerously stubborn heads? In the fall of 2010, Faroque Ahmed, a Pakistani-born Virginia man was arrested for plotting to bomb the Washington area Metro system. His nefarious scheme was foiled by FBI agents whom he thought were Al Qaeda operatives. That's because the agents apparently *looked like him*; but they were the *good* guys.

When former NPR commentator Juan Williams lost his job last fall for having a bad case of foot-in-mouth disease for publicly expressing the fear he experiences when observing Muslims in this country who identify themselves *first* as Muslim, I thought to myself, "If only it were just that easy." Not only can people never be painted with the same brush – no matter what faith, nationality or race – but his misdirected tendency to profile is an exercise in futility. Being a terrorist is a sick, extremist mindset; *not* a religion. Whatever we consider an American to be and look like; I believe they will come at us . . . as us.

Like every other American, I salute and am grateful to President Obama for his steadfastness and courage in ordering the mission which snuffed out Osama bin Laden. As a former Navy airman, I am extremely proud of and grateful to the US Navy Seals who so brilliantly and fearlessly carried out the mission.

It also feels very serendipitous that the annihilation of the world's number one terrorist was carried out one year to the date of the May 1, 2010 incident in Times Square.

The head of the cockroach has been squashed, but terrorists – like cockroaches - are cunning and tricky to wipe out completely. But, I believe it can be achieved. With the head gone, I suspect the other roaches are looking over their shoulders a bit more.

With bin Laden dead, I believe we can capitalize on this opportunity to hunt, neutralize or exterminate Al Qaeda once and for all; doubling our efforts both here at home and wherever our enemies are in the world.

I believe we must fight terrorism all over the world and be supportive of those Islamic nations and movements that crave democracy – like Egypt, Libya & Syria. The future of freedom in the world can only happen when people have the free will to decide their leaders and the type of society that they want.

Perhaps when you've been a part of war, you see things a bit differently. As someone who has served our country in the armed forces, I believe that the threat of terrorism will continue to hang over our heads as long as we continue to engage in political wars. Vietnam. Iraq. Afghanistan. No matter who is in power in the White House – Democrats or Republicans. How can we continue to fight and lose precious American lives with one hand tied behind our backs? That hand being the clear resolve to *win*.

So, as the political wars continue, the terrorist threats continue. And escalate. Bombs hidden in computer cartridges shipped on cargo planes headed to the U.S. are among the latest pernicious plans to be thwarted. Detonation devices have also been found to be hidden in body cavities of terrorist family members. To them, such cold-blooded sacrifices are all part of Jihad. Terrorists' twisted plots to destroy us are growing more vicious and devious.

In the meantime, we must remain vigilant, respect each other and have each others' back. Just as I have always taught my children, don't be afraid of getting involved. Look out for your brother and your sister – which includes those brothers and sisters who are not related to you.

After everything that has transpired in my life, in my city and in my country – I believe it is my mission to do just that because we are indeed a community of "one."

Because I believe more strongly than ever that we are our brothers' – and sisters' – keepers, I have made a decision which I would like to share with you here. I have decided to explore running for Congress from my district in the Upper Hudson Valley of New York. Why would I want to take on such a headache, right?

A couple of reasons. First, I think it is in my DNA to help other people whenever and however I can. That's just me. Secondly, I think I could bring a little common sense to that esteemed branch of our government. Maybe a little too esteemed. People get voted into office and far too often seem to forget where they came from; and why they ran for office in the first place. Aren't our representatives there to serve us? To put in the time to make life better for the people of their respective districts in particular, and people in the country in general? I thought so; but, somehow that doesn't always seem to be the case. I'd like the opportunity to put in that time for those of in the Hudson Valley. I don't know about you, but I'm pretty tired of lip service.

Like our President, I believe that bi-partisanship, working together – regardless of party affiliation – is the *only* way to solve our problems. As Americans, *aren't we all ultimately on the same team?*

In closing, I want to thank all of you who are reading this for your support of me. For your kind words, your thoughts, and prayers. Collectively, we can *do* this, you know. Life shouldn't be taken for granted, 'cause all we've got is right now. And, each other.

chapter seven

Dolly Parton thanking Duane for his heroic actions.

Hello Dolly!

Times Square is often referred to as the "Crossroads of the World." Accurate moniker. From my little corner, I am privileged to watch and sometimes meet and mingle with people from all walks of life – tourists from every corner of the globe, hurried native New Yorkers, and of course those we consider to be "the rich and the famous."

One of my favorite people in the world is the delightful Dolly Parton. I met Dolly earlier in 2010 when she was involved with the Broadway production of "9 to 5: The Musical." I know you remember when Dolly starred in the movies back in the 80s. This pretty lady is seriously talented and wrote the music and lyrics for this production.

My stand is right across the street from the Marquis Theatre, so "seeing stars" coming and going is almost routine. One day, when I spotted Dolly exiting the stage door, I asked her manager if we could take a picture together. She's gracious, so she obliged. We snapped it right there. As a bonus, Dolly's assistant ran out a bit later and must have liked what she saw on my table because she bought an armful of merchandise!

A couple of weeks after "the incident," my next-door neighbor vendors excitedly informed me that Dolly Parton had actually come to 45th Street looking for me! *And, I wasn't there! I think I just ran to use the restroom.*

Later that evening, a guy came running through the breezeway at the Minskoff Theater, identified himself as Dolly Parton's driver and said, "Dolly wants to talk to you!" So, I ran like a bat out of hell over to the car with him, trying to contain my excitement. There was no media. No entourage. Just Dolly.

She was flashing that megawatt smile as she stepped out of the back seat, extending her arms. "Darlin', I just wanted to come by and give you a big ole' hug and tell you how proud I am of you. God Bless you!" Through a stroke of luck, I happened to have a disposable camera in my pocket. Bam! The moment was frozen for me forever. It meant so much to me that someone of her stature remembered me, even making the effort to find me – twice - just to say "Thank you." Special.

Even though I had received a proclamation from Governor Patterson's office after the incident, I had never met him personally. One day, about a week or so after that, his office called to say the Governor wanted to come down. So, days later, here is David Patterson on 45th Street just to say "hi" and "thank you."

After introductions, we just stood there shooting the breeze as though we were old friends. We discovered we have a mutual friend – a good brother named Charles Knox LaSister. Knox and I were classmates at Boston University. As it turns out, he and Governor Patterson grew up together on Long Island.

Since the Governor has even poked fun of himself and his visual disability on national TV (*Saturday Night Live*), I'm sure he won't mind when I say that talking with him was like having a "Stevie Wonder moment." Let's just say it's a tad disconcerting when you're trying to have a conversation.

Especially if you're not used to talking to him, I guess. You're not quite sure if he's looking at you or not; or exactly how *you* should be looking at *him* because of the eye issue. Of course, we took a picture together.

My brothas – those of you who are also married will understand this: I had to ditch the Governor. My wife was waiting for me at the 23rd Street Pier. We were guests on the Delta's boatride. (For those of you who are not familiar with the world of Black Greeks, Delta Sigma Theta is a century-old, revered Black sorority.) When I explained this to Governor Patterson's press person, he totally understood. I made the boat.

Linda and I were both a little stunned – but happily overwhelmed by the love our fellow guests showed us when we stepped on board. Applause broke out from nowhere. And, again, I was thanked for being a "hero."

I made a special new friend that evening. On the boat was Helen Williams, mother of actress Vanessa Williams. (The apple didn't fall far from *that* tree!) We talked and joked about me being her "bag man." Two years prior, Helen hosted a "bag party" for her Links Chapter (another long-established, well-respected Black woman's organization) in Westchester. She was the chapter president and invited me to supply the bags. We've been friends ever since!

The new, life-long friends I made at the FBI Citizens Academy are another blessing. The forty-four members of the 2010 class included educators, judges, ministers, attorneys, executives, former cops, writers and me. We were each selected for the elite program because someone thought of us as leaders in our respective communities. We graduated on November 22, 2010. I was elected Class President and had the honor of giving our graduation address.

Over the 10 week course, members of the FBI Citizens Academy were instructed in FBI practices and its core motivating beliefs: Fidelity. Bravery. Integrity. Principles critical to all our lives. We spent time at a shooting range and were schooled in the proper – and safe – use of weapons. Hopefully, none of us will ever have a reason to draw or use a weapon. If such a circumstance is ever presented, however; it is better to be knowledgeable.

It was during the Citizens Academy classes that I met a helluva guy who I am proud to call my friend, retired FBI agent, Joaquin "Jack" Garcia. He is my "brother from another mother." We're both big, tall guys; both born in September 1952. Maybe you saw Joaquin's profile on *60 Minutes* a couple of years back. He is the FBI agent who posed as a wiseguy for two and a half years, taking down the infamous Gambino family in one of the biggest Mafia roundups in history. Joaquin, who is Cuban-American, was so convincing as his Italian gangster alter-ego Jack Falcone, Gambino family ring leader Greg DePalma invited him into the fold – offering the mob's highest honor: being "made." You've all seen gangster movies and TV shows, so you know becoming a sworn-in member of the Mafia involves taking someone out. Of course, the sting went down before the initiation could be carried out. Joaquin, who is one ballsy guy, wrote about the experience in his book, "Making Jack Falcone." The movie version, starring Benicio Del Toro, will be released by Paramount Pictures in 2012.

While acknowledgement and attention from public people is pretty cool, the most heart-warming moments for me have been when regular people from throughout the country and even around the world – perfect strangers - stop by "Duane's of Times Square" just to say "hi," shake my hand, take a picture with me or give me a hug. One lady pressed $20 into my palm and said, "I saw you on TV, so I just wanted to come by and buy something from you." She hadn't even looked at the merchandise.

Sometimes someone would say, "My father or grandfather was a Vietnam vet."

"My brother died in Vietnam."

"My son is in Afghanistan."

"My daughter is serving her second tour of duty."

"God bless you."

Or simply, "Thank you for what you did for us."

No, thank *you*!

Chapter_eight

On The Street

Scores of people from all walks of life have approached me at my stand in Times Square to say 'thanks' and express their gratitude for what I did on May 1st. I never tire of it – and appreciate meeting each and every one of them. Following are just a few of the people who I have met.

Only in Times Square: Obama, Palin, and Clinton with
Duane Jackson. Smile!

chapter_nine

But Words Are Powerful

Thank you, my friends.

May 4, 2010
Hi Duane—
I just wanted to tell you how honored I feel to have just met you on my visit to Times Square only a week ago (my friend and I bought handbags from you and you gave us scarves--1 for each of us and 1 for our friend who was hospitalized) only to see you on the news regarding the recent incident. Of all the things I saw in New York City that weekend, you were the most impressive, and this incident proves that you are as special as I thought you were!
God bless you,
Sandy
Wallingford, PA

Duane,
Mary and I think that the mayor took the wrong people out to dinner - YOU guys (who watch the streets EVERY day) were the REAL HEROS. We're proud of you!!! See you soon.

Love you Brother,
Mike & Mary

Way to go Duane.... Our Hero. Loved seeing you on all the different news and entertainment shows. All your friends at Hagedorn are very proud to know you. Keep up the good work.
All the best,
Mary Courtney
PS: I sent the article about you from the Staten Island paper to Sandy in NC.
Mr. Jackson, my name is Michael Baer and I'm an Emergency Medical Technician with the New York City Fire Department. I just wanted to say thank you for not only your service to this great country but for what you did the other day. Stay safe, sir.
Thank you for being a great American,
Michael Baer

Good morning,
This is the first message I've received for you, but believe there will be many more!
Thanks for being so vigilant and speaking up. You did a great thing!
By the way: You were mentioned several times on Opera radio(XM 156) this morning.
Carol Engle
Silver Spring, MD

THANK YOU, Smokey!!!!!!!!!!!!!!!!!
Shirley
New York, NY

Thanks so much for being an American Hero.
Suzy from Minneapolis, Minnesota. 5.8.10

Mr. Jackson, My sister and I want to express our gratitude for you taking your valuable time to talk to us. Great job with preventing an otherwise unpleasant experience that could have hurt a lot of people. May God's blessings continue to be with you.

Lou Cain

Thank you to our hero.   It's true what they say if you see something, say something.

Mari

Duane, thank you again both for being there and reacting when it counted last week. And a big thank you for your service in the Vietnam War!! We all appreciate it.....and thanks for the picture too..I love it!!.........
JaneDuane –

I'm attaching a picture of you and my father, RT Savage, who came to visit NYC this past weekend from Richmond, VA. He was so glad to see you, get a picture taken, and THANK YOU for what you're doing for our country. You are demonstrating how one person can make a big difference.

Thanks!
Rachael (and RT) Savage

Hi Duane,
It was a pleasure meeting you on Sunday. Attached are the photos we took. I emailed the photos to all of my family back west and we are all very proud of you.
When we get back to Great Falls, Montana, we will email you a photo of my Dad with the t-shirt you gave him.
The scarf I bought is keeping me very warm on these blustery days!
Kelly and Mark Schumacher

Hi Dad,
We found Duane Jackson today just where we thought he'd be – right in front of the Marriott hotel. We immediately recognized him from seeing him on the news.
We introduced ourselves and presented him with the Wolf Creek, Montana t-shirt you gave us to give to him (see photo #46). He was very appreciative and reciprocated by giving us a t-shirt to give to you (see photo #47). The t-shirt says *"I saw something…so I said something"* and there is a photo of

him next to an American flag. He is a very nice fellow and is humble about thwarting the possible bomb disaster. He said a couple of days ago he was taken to the FBI office where he spoke with President Obama on the telephone. Obama thanked him for alerting the police of the SUV.
Duane pointed out to us exactly where the SUV was parked. In photo #49 I am standing in the exact spot.
Kelly and Mark, reporting from Times Square

Hi Duane,
I stopped at your corner over the week-end. I was from Chicago and you told me about your Wilmette roommate.
Anyhow, you said you wanted me to email the picture my husband took of you and I, so here it is.
I was so excited to meet you that I forgot to even at what you were selling. We might be back in New York in July and if we come, I will return to your table and actually look and buy this time!!
Take care,
Patti McEneaney

My name is Jeannie Thibault and I am from Goodrich, Michigan....
Thanks again for saying something when you saw something:)

Mr. Jackson,
Attached are the pictures we took with you in NYC on Saturday, May 8th. Thank you so much for taking the time to speak with us and to take a picture. It was a pleasure to meet you!

There are two pictures attached. The one with you and the girls the names are Allyson Bayer, Makayla Lewis and Janette Lewis. The other one is with you and Joe Rohrer. Didn't know if you wanted names or not.

Again it was a great pleasure to meet you and thank you so much for your kindness and your dedication to the people of NYC and the USA!

Take Care and God Bless,
Janette Lewis :o)

Duane,
As promised, I have forwarded the pictures we took in New York. I have had such a fun time telling everyone about the "famous" purse vendor and hero. I so enjoyed your stories. You were a great addition to my holiday in New York.

Thanks so much,
Jo Anne Brown

Dear Mr. Duane,
Want to say it was nice meeting you and thanks again for the heroic act you did. God used you to save again many lives!
Any time you come to Abbeville, Louisiana come visit us!
The Kasperski's

Hi Duane,
My Dad was thrilled with the t-shirt you gave us for him. He'll cherish the gift from a real American hero. Attached is a thank you note he made for you. Thanks again, and we hope to see you again.
Kelly and Mark Schumacher

Hi Smokey,

Just a word of CONGRATULATIONS for your brave deed! You certainly are to be commended for showing our president, nation & the world that we are attentive to our environment 24/7!!! Go Black Veteran. I hope that our illustrious mayor realizes that VENDORS are intelligent people who are in business. We need You!!

PEACE,

Lynnette Brinson CFA'75
NETBRIN

Hi Duane,
I enjoyed meeting you and send you all the best luck. I hope you have a great time in Milwaukee in August. Thank you for the beautiful pink scarf.

We absolutely loved NYC and everyone was just as friendly there as here in the midwest.

Lucy Husting

Sir,

Thank you again for your clear thinking and quick action on 1 May 2010. As I told you today, I have always been proud to be a Soldier, but I stood even taller the day we found out it was a Vietnam Vet who made the call. Best wishes to you.

I will send a few more photos to you.

CSM Jeffrey Mellinger
U.S. Army

Dear Duane,
It was a pleasure and an honor to meet you today.
Thank you very much for the T-shirt and wallet you gave me for my birthday.

I look forward to seeing you next time I'm in New York.
And if you're ever in Israel please contact me.
Thank you again,

Ohad Alon

Duane,
If I've done this correctly, you should be receiving this email along with the attached photo you were gracious enough to allow us to take on July 4th. It was a special trip for the four of us, but we all agreed the highlight was meeting you.
Thanks again for what you did and are still doing for our country.

Gregg McPherson
Platte City, MO

Gday Mr. Jackson (Duane?),
I finally made it back to Australia and here are those photos I promised you. Did you ever make it on to TV? It was heaps of fun meeting you (even under the bizarre circumstances) and I LOVE my wrap. Thank you, that was very generous of you.

If you ever make it to Cairns, Australia you will have a tour guide waiting for you!
Cheers,
Pam Raymond

Here is a true American hero. This is the gentleman who saw the Pathfinder parked at Times Square in NYC. You the man Duane. America (and Canada) thank you.
Scott Burgoyne

Hello Duane Jackson and Rick Samuel. This is the pic we took during training. Once Again GOD Bless you and thank you for "saying something".
Darryl Thompson

Duane,
It was sincerely my pleasure to have met you and talked to you last evening..... You are articulate, energetic, exciting, and one hell of a nice guy!!!!! Hopefully I will meet up with you again on the streets of New York City......

Regards

Ron Regen

Duane with Norman Reedus of "The Walking Dead."

Duane and his Spiritual Advisors

Chapter Ten

9/11 Never Forget

chapter_eleven

Law Enforcement Photos

Duane shooting an M5 during training at the Citizens' Academy.

The 2010 graduating class of the FBI Citizens' Academy.

Duane Jackson addressing the FBI Citizens' Academy.

Duane and Joaquin "Big Jack" Garcia, a former undercover FBI agent
that successfully infiltrated the mob.

New York FBI Director Janice K. Fedarcyk presenting Duane with his
certificate of graduation from the 2010 Citizens' Academy.

Duane with FBI agents Stacy Diamond and Rickard Kolko

Duane with Ron Regen

Duane on duty at his stand in Times Square with Cheryl,
one of the beat cops, atop Roy.

Greatest Fan

Chapter Twelve

Politician Photos

Duane with the Admiral of the Fleet during Fleet Week in NYC.

Duane Jackson attending a Veteran's ceremony in 1998…

…and a more recent photo, again attending a Veteran's ceremony.

chapter_thirteen

Acknowledgments

Duane Jackson posing with NYC Mayor Michael
Bloomberg near his Times Square stand.

Duane and former NYC Mayor Rudolph Giuliani.

Duane and former New York State Governor Mario Cuomo.

Duane and Ron Reagan, Jr., the son of former President Ronald Reagan.

Duane and former Senator Fred Thompson, also known
for his role on Law and Order.

Duane and Senator Lindsey Graham

have had the honor of being recognized by many organizations on the local, state, and federal level. There have been too many to mention; following are some that are special to me.

Duane Jackson being recognized by the NY Mets at Citifield.

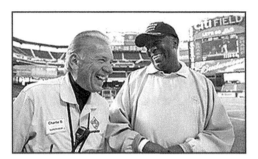

Duane with Charlie Demoli at Citifield.

Duane addressing the crowd at the Town of Cortlandt,
NY Memorial Day ceremony in 2010.

U.S. Department of Justice
Federal Bureau of Investigation
New York Division

Presents this certificate to

Duane M. Jackson

on this day

November 23, 2010

*For successfully completing
the FBI Citizens' Academy program
and demonstrating a commitment to the FBI mission*

Assistant Director In Charge

Robert S. Mueller, III
Director

The certificate Duane received upon his completion
of the 2010 FBI Citizens' Academy.

U.S. Department of Justice

Federal Bureau of Investigation

Office of the Director   *Washington, D.C. 20535-0001*

November 23, 2010

Mr. Duane M. Jackson
Federal Bureau of Investigation
New York Division

Dear Mr. Jackson:

Congratulations on your graduation from the FBI Citizens' Academy. I appreciate the commitment you have shown by making this significant investment of time away from your work and family to gain a deeper understanding of the FBI and its mission for the American people. I hope you found the experience to be rewarding.

You have already shown your commitment to the FBI and its mission. I hope I can impose upon you to continue displaying that same dedication in the following three ways.

First, continue to serve as a role model in your community. Continue to be a leader in your field. Continue to help us protect your community and use the valuable perspectives you have gained as a Citizens' Academy graduate. What you have learned makes you a strong asset in the fight against terrorism and crime. With the knowledge you have gained in the time you have devoted to this program you are better attuned to the indicators associated with crimes from terrorism and espionage to fraud and organized crime.

Second, continue to support the Citizens' Academy. Recommend your peers for the program. Take part in the activities of the national and local Citizens' Academy alumni associations.

Third, serve as ambassadors for the FBI. Spread the word. Do for others what we tried to do for you: demystify the FBI and share what you have learned about the vital role our Special Agents, analysts and support employees play in protecting all people in the United States and Americans around the world. The way the FBI is perceived matters a great deal. It can mean the difference between someone coming forward with a vital piece of information that could prevent crime or the next terrorist attack, or not.

While the support and understanding of the general public are essential to our success, Citizens' Academy alumni in particular have made many contributions to the FBI's mission. We thank you for your support now and in the future, and we look forward to working with you in the coming years to protect our communities and our country.

Sincerely yours,

Robert S. Mueller, III
Director

Letter of congratulations Duane received from FBI Director Robert Mueller upon completion of the Citizens' Academy.

KIRSTEN E. GILLIBRAND
NEW YORK

UNITED STATES SENATOR

May 4, 2010

Mr. Duane Jackson
6 Lake Drive
Buchanan, New York 10511

Dear Mr. Jackson,

On behalf of the people of New York, I would like to thank you for your extraordinary citizenship and service to the community on the evening of Saturday May 1, 2010. By spotting the suspicious SUV in the Times Square area, and proactively following through by alerting the New York Police Department authorities, you did a service to us all.

Thank you for seeing something and saying something. Your vigilance and quick judgment protected the safety and lives of countless New Yorkers, and the people of New York are forever grateful. As a Vietman War veteran especially, your extended service to our nation—then and now—is recognized and duly appreciated.

With deepest gratitude, I am

Sincerely yours,

Thank you for your outstanding service to our country and your courage.

Kirsten E. Gillibrand
United States Senator

NOT PRINTED AT GOVERNMENT EXPENSE

Personalized letter from New York State Senator Kirsten Gillibrand thanking Duane for his heroic actions on May 1, 2010.

Department of Veterans Affairs

Certificate of Appreciation

Presented to

Duane M. Jackson

*In recognition and appreciation of your personal
commitment and dedication
to provide the best possible service to our
Nation's Veterans and to the
People of the United States of America.*

Given By

VA Hudson Valley Health Care System
On this
9th Day of November 2010

Gerald F. Culliton, MPA
Director

Duane received this certificate from the Director of the VA Hudson Valley Health
Care System in recognition of his ongoing contributions to Veteran issues.

Duane was interviewed and honore by all media – television, newspaper – even radio. National radio personality Nick Cannon presented Duane with his "Cannon's Hero Award" for seeing something and saying something.

School News...

The Times Square Hero Who Saved the Day
By Dylan G. Daly

On Mother's Day, I went to New York City with my whole family and met a true American hero. The day before was my First Holy Communion, so my older sister, Cherie, was in town from Los Angeles, where she lives. My parents had gotten tickets to see "The Addams Family" on Broadway to reward me for doing good work in school. Before the show, we were walking in Times Square and we ran into Duane Jackson, a street vendor for more than 13 years. My mother recognized him from the front page of the newspaper. My parents introduced me to him so I could learn that there are real heroes in the world. Mr. Jackson is a U.S. Navy veteran, having served in Vietnam. He is originally from San Francisco, and told us that he moved to New York and met his wife in Brooklyn. He now lives with her in northern Westchester.

Last weekend, Duane was selling his usual merchandise of purses and handbags in Times Square when he noticed an SUV parked in a bus lane with its lights flashing. He went over to the car and saw that the keys were still in it. He was suspicious and alerted the police who went over to the vehicle and found smoke coming out of it. Police and FBI officials later discovered that there had been explosives in the van that could have caused major damage and a huge loss of innocent lives. They later caught the man who had left that dangerous car there trying to flee the country.

Duane told me and my family that he had been personally thanked by entertainment celebrities including Dolly Parton, Jeff Goldblum, and Nathan Lane. And while we were there, people started lining up just to say thank you and take a picture with him. He was friendly and personable to all while remaining gracious and, above all, modest. We later learned that he had gotten a thank-you phone call from President Obama and a standing ovation from the Mets and thousands of their fans at Citi Field. He has been on a lot of television interviews since his heroic act that saved our wonderful City of New York. There should be more heroes like Duane Jackson. It was a pleasure and an honor for me to meet him.

School reporter Dylan Daly's account of meeting Duane at his Times Square stand, where he thanked Duane for his action on May first.

chapter_fifteen

News Clippings

The iconic image now associated with the would-be bombing of Times Square on May 1, 2010 if not for the heroic action of Times Square vendor Duane Jackson.

Duane Jackson: TIMES SQUARE HERO

BY BOB HOPKINS

The pop! pop! pop! that Duane Jackson heard as he stared in the window of an illegally parked SUV was nothing compared to the roar of an A7A Corsair II fighter leaving the deck of the U.S.S. *Ranger*. Jackson, who served on the *Ranger* as she patrolled off the Vietnam coast, sensed however that he was in danger as did the New York City police officer near him. This was not your usual Saturday night in Times Square.

Jackson, a California native who had morphed into a New Yorker, enlisted the Navy after high school. He served on the *Ranger* from 1970-73 with two tours of duty on Yankee Station. He was on board for Operation Linebacker II, the December 1972 bombing of North Vietnam that forced Hanoi back to the bargaining table.

After the war, Jackson came to the East Coast for college, married, had two children, and worked a series of jobs from advertising to city planning in New York City and Maryland. He was between jobs when he found out that he was eligible as a disabled veteran for a New York City vendor's license.

In 1989, Jackson obtained his permit and set up shop in midtown Manhattan, with a second location in the Wall Street district. He quickly became embroiled in the attempt by city officials and the Fifth Avenue Merchants Association to ban vendors from selling their wares in the midtown area. They tried to curb or repeal a post Civil War law that permitted disabled veterans to hawk their wares anywhere in the state of New York without interference from local laws or ordinances. It was during this battle, which lasted several years, that Jackson met John Rowan, a veteran activist who today is VVA's National President. Rowan encouraged Jackson to form a VVA Chapter, as it would add more firepower for his cause.

Jackson heeded that advice and started VVA Chapter 817, which was primarily composed of disabled Vietnam veterans with vendor's licenses. He was elected president, an office he still holds. Through the efforts of Jackson, Chapter members, and their political allies, compromises were negotiated that kept the disabled veterans in business and allowed them to retain many of their prime midtown locations.

Jackson was selling ties near Wall Street in 1993 when a truck bomb exploded in the World Trade Center. He was in a similar location when the 9/11 attack occurred. He used his vehicle to help transport fire fighters and their equipment to a battalion staging area right after the planes hit.

On Saturday morning, May 1, Jackson arrived a little later than usual at his 45th Street location. "It was a beautiful spring day," he said. "Around 6:30 p.m. it got real busy, with people coming in for the 8 p.m. shows. I noticed an SUV illegally parked where the buses turn into the Marriott. It had its flashers on, with no one in the car. I went over and looked in and noticed the keys were in the ignition and the engine was running."

At this point, a mounted policeman came on the scene. "He asked me if I knew whose car it was," Jackson said. "I told him 'no. We know all the cops and they know us. I noticed the car was smoking. A call went in for the fire department. There was a lot of smoke in the car, and a cop and I were looking in when we heard the pops. That's when everyone started running. I ran part way up the block and stayed there."

Fire equipment quickly arrived, followed by the bomb squad. Jackson remained in the area and was interviewed by two city detectives. He wasn't allowed to retrieve his merchandise until the next morning.

Jackson plays down his part in the incident. He minimizes any talk of being a hero. "The heroes are guys like Sully Sullenberger who landed that plane on the river," he said.

Duane Jackson has asked that any money offered for his interviews or appearances be donated to Vietnam Veterans of America to continue our work with Vietnam veterans and to support today's new veterans.

"We have to take care of our own," he said. "It is our responsibility to speak out for those who didn't make it home and to help those who made it back." ∎

Duane's account of what he saw and did on May 2, 2010 printed in a Veteran's publication.

The Daily News honoring a Decade of Heroes, including Duane Jackson.

News headlines from the killing of Osama bin Laden on May 1, 2011; ironically, it was exactly one year previously that Duane Jackson thwarted a would-be bomber from detonating an SUV loaded with enough explosives to kill thousands of people and cause catastrophic damage to Times Square.

Chapter_sixteen

CEO/Business People

Duane with Michael Eisner, former Chief Executive Officer of Disney.

Steve Forbes, Chairman and Editor-in-Chief of Forbes Media, with Duane in Times Square.

Duane with the king of bonds, William Gross (both coincidentally from California).

chapter seventeen

Celebrity Photos

P eople from all walks of life come through Times Square on a daily basis – including celebrities. And I enjoy getting get my picture taken with all of them!

Anthony Anderson, one of the hot young actors.

The ladies may know him from All My Children, but for men,
he is most recognizable from Bonanza. It's a gender thing.

Model and actor Taye Diggs and his stage actress wife Idina Menzel
with Duane.

Harvey Fierstein, one of the best-known stage and film actors around.

Luis Guzman, a terrific character actor.

Terrence Howard. A little Hustle and Flow, anyone?

Don King, promoter extraordinaire.

The legendary Jerry Lewis.

George Lopez, one of the funniest men on television.

Chris Matthews of MSNBC's Hardball with Chris Matthews.

S. Epatha Merkerson, best known from Law and Order.

Dolly Parton. Although her photo appears in another chapter of this book, I had to include her here as well because she is that special!

Funny man Bob Saget.

Steven Shirripa, best known for his role Bobby Bacala on The Sopranos.

Duane and Glenn Cook flanking NY Mets legend Darryl Strawberry.

Cornel West, Princeton professor and civil rights activist.

Dexter actor David Zayas.

Visit
www.MayFirstTheBook.com
to access links to publications, videos, interviews,
testimonials, and current updates.

A special acknowledgment to the VA Montrose Hospital and the Friars of the Atonement at Graymoor, and my Times Square neighbors The Marriott Marquis and Viacom, especially all those kind enough to present me with a banner signed with congratulatory messages. Peace and love to them all.

Duane with Jimmy Fallon

Duane with Alfred Molina.

chapter eighteen

Running for Public Office and You Don't Know What You Don't Know?

t all started for me in the late' 60s in my high school history class on a beautiful California day. It was the presidential primary season. Nelson Rockefeller walked into my classroom at Centennial High School in Compton, California. I was on the debating team so I was up on the issues of the day, but what first stood out to me was here was Nelson Rockefeller, the grandson of John D. Rockefeller of Standard Oil! I had read about him in my history book, *Money and Monopolies*. It was 3 years after the Watts Riot and the nation's loss of President Kennedy. Bobby and Martin were yet to happen. As I have thought back to that day, over the last 45 years, that was my beginning, trying to understand the political world and my place in It. Over the next two years of high school, my debating partner and I would tackle issues on both sides, pro and con. My debating partner was Everson Esters. He was also president of the senior class and I was a member of the school senate and his right-hand man. Those years in Compton saw the election of the first black mayor and the first black superintendent of schools Dr. Alonso Crim; also Everson's father was a minister with a good-sized Baptist church, so we talked about politics all the time. An interesting side note was that Everson and I both worked at Disneyland July 1969 when America landed on the moon. I'll get back to that story later. After graduation, I joined the Navy and Everson went to Ripon College in Wisconsin, the birthplace of the Republican Party. After leaving the Navy, I came home and started college at the state university. Everson had dropped out in his second year to work on the George McGovern campaign for President. Everson and I hooked up again after McGovern lost to Nixon.

Everson would talk to me about his experience with the McGovern campaign and being on the East Coast. I was both amazed and intrigued by what he talked about and how he wanted to go to college back East, so much so that I decided to leave southern California and continue my education at Boston University. 1973 Boston Mayor Kevin White, an old-school politician. I can remember being in the south end of Boston looking at some empty lots and unfinished apartment housing thinking to myself, "If there was a riot in Boston like Watts in California,..." only to be told that the abandoned buildings were the result of cutbacks in urban development funding, i.e.--Massachusetts was the only state to vote against Nixon in 1972!!!

My first internship was at the Dorchester Area Planning Council, a part of the old Model Cities program, where I first learned about politics, money and voting blocks. Back in 1968 with Rockefeller in my history class, he had been visiting a Model Cities development across from my high school. One of my comments on the campaign trail from 2012 was, "Community development must be anchored in the community so no matter who is in power, your development is based on local resources and blood, sweat and tears of your own community. Why I ran for Congress: Having majored in City Planning in Boston, studied Transportation Planning in Washington, D.C., with the summer internship program at Georgia Tech and the experience of being a Capital Budget Planner for the largest school system in the U.S., New York City, I wanted to put my planning experience at work in a Congressional District. How do we change the current political system? First off, we have to have ordinary people seeking public office, especially at the Congressional level. We cannot leave it to career politicians with special interests and well connected; change must come from the ground level up. When the government we have elected fails to serve the needs of the people, it is our duty to change that government. That's why I ran for Congress.

Disneyland 1969

As I mentioned before, Everson and I worked at the Magic Kingdom, along with Tim Crim, son of Dr. Alonso Crim, who would later reform the Atlanta school system after leaving his mark on the Compton school system which

I graduated from. Also, my fellow Boy Scout member, Raymond Kearns, we were the four amigos working at Walt Disney's dreamland which I embraced. Not only is it an effective amusement park, but inspiration for planning tomorrow's cities, which led me to study city planning five years later at Boston University. Mr. Disney's forward thinking and design were my influences on how we could make American cities and towns just as good, by thinking outside the box.

My history of being a boy scout, working at Disneyland, an airman in the Navy, studying City Planning in Boston and in D.C. and working in Capital Budget Planning in N.Y.C., gave me the skills and understanding in how I can make my community better. In 1978, Everson and I hooked back up in Washington, D.C.; he was working at the Democratic National Committee (DNC), reporting to the chairman, Detroit Mayor Coleman Young. Everson got me a job working for then-Mayor of D.C., Walter Washington in his campaign, my first taste of the political world. Unfortunately he lost to Marion Berry, and as they say, the rest is history.

The beautiful and historical Hudson Valley, where I had lived since 1995, had been infected in 2010 by a Republican named Nan Hayworth and the Tea Party. The valley, which had been center-leaning under Congressman Hamilton Fish, Jr., turned to the far right with the election of Dr. Nan Hayworth and I could not let that stand in my valley. That's why I ran for Congress; she and the Tea Party had to go. The Congressional campaign took me to the cities of <u>Poughkeepsie</u>, Beacon, Newburgh, Middletown and Bedford. Up and down the valley.

In my political opinion today, we have created a system both on the left and the right of people, institutions, businesses and multi-national organizations that game the system, that game the American people, from oil subsidies to big oil to civil service pension programs. We have developed a system in government that we cannot sustain, that must be reformed.

But you don't know what you don't know. My Congressional race had four other candidates who I salute for their courage to get involved in the process: Dr. Richard Becker, Councilman of the town of Courtlandt Manor, New York, Mayor Matthew Alexander, Mayor Tom Wilson and Sean Patrick Maloney, who won by being connected to former president Bill Clinton. Let's hope he can connect to the community he serves. The 18th Congressional District I ran in unfortunately had the boundaries changed three months after I entered the race. Should I have dropped out? No, in hindsight, what an experience it was! The people at the grassroots level that I met, the local and regional politicians, the community organizers and the men and women of the clergy all became a family to me. Most of them I'm in contact with today and will probably be lifelong friends with.

On March 19, 2012, I was elected to serve as a Village Trustee for the Village of Buchanan, New York, in the Hudson Valley. That experience, campaigning locally, meeting your neighbors that you know and didn't know, is a great testament to the words of former Speaker of the House, Tip O'Neill, who always stated that all politics are local. It is my hope as I continue to serve on the village board, that my life experiences will guide me in doing the right thing for the people of Buchanan, New York. I was elected both by Democrats, Republicans and Independents. If our democracy continues it will be by those of us who get involved and get connected at the local level. The pessimism and disenfranchisement of people about how their government works can only be changed by more involvement of the citizens, hence the phrase, we must take our government back from those who want to control it for their own selfish needs and wants. My story to those who will read this book is a simple one: there's no substitute for involvement, you've got to be involved to change anything in the political world. And that change comes about brick by brick at the foundation of our democracy. The events that have shaped my life, moving from California to Boston, witnessing the attack on the World Trade Center, owning a business on Wall Street and seeing the financial juggling that was done in the late '90s and the 2000s by big banks and brokerage houses…change must come if we are to survive as a democracy, not as a two-class society of the haves and the have-nots. My belief of trusting in a higher power, the spiritualness of the universe that connects all will always be front and center in how I approach Life on Life's terms. God bless all of you who will read this book, let it be a strength and an inspiration to you that when life knocks you down, there will be those that will help you up, and those that will not. But it is indeed incumbent on you, the individual, to get up, dust yourself off, and go forward. We all are indeed our brother's keeper.